Seven Hermetic Principles

Three Initiates

Kessinger Publishing's Rare Reprints

Thousands of Scarce and Hard-to-Find Books
on These and other Subjects!

- Americana
- Ancient Mysteries
- Animals
- Anthropology
- Architecture
- Arts
- Astrology
- Bibliographies
- Biographies & Memoirs
- Body, Mind & Spirit
- Business & Investing
- Children & Young Adult
- Collectibles
- Comparative Religions
- Crafts & Hobbies
- Earth Sciences
- Education
- Ephemera
- Fiction
- Folklore
- Geography
- Health & Diet
- History
- Hobbies & Leisure
- Humor
- Illustrated Books
- Language & Culture
- Law
- Life Sciences
- Literature
- Medicine & Pharmacy
- Metaphysical
- Music
- Mystery & Crime
- Mythology
- Natural History
- Outdoor & Nature
- Philosophy
- Poetry
- Political Science
- Science
- Psychiatry & Psychology
- Reference
- Religion & Spiritualism
- Rhetoric
- Sacred Books
- Science Fiction
- Science & Technology
- Self-Help
- Social Sciences
- Symbolism
- Theatre & Drama
- Theology
- Travel & Explorations
- War & Military
- Women
- Yoga
- *Plus Much More!*

We kindly invite you to view our catalog list at:
http://www.kessinger.net

CHAPTER II.

THE SEVEN HERMETIC PRINCIPLES.

"The Principles of Truth are Seven; he who knows these, understandingly, possesses the Magic Key before whose touch all the Doors of the Temple fly open."— *The Kybalion.*

The Seven Hermetic Principles, upon which the entire Hermetic Philosophy is based, are as follows:

   I. THE PRINCIPLE OF MENTALISM.

  II. THE PRINCIPLE OF CORRESPONDENCE.

 III. THE PRINCIPLE OF VIBRATION.

 IV. THE PRINCIPLE OF POLARITY.

  V. THE PRINCIPLE OF RHYTHM.

VI. THE PRINCIPLE OF CAUSE
AND EFFECT.
VII. THE PRINCIPLE OF GENDER.

These Seven Principles will be discussed
and explained as we proceed with these les-
sons. A short explanation of each, how-
ever, may as well be given at this point.

I. THE PRINCIPLE OF MENTALISM.

"THE ALL is MIND; The Universe is Mental."—
The Kybalion.

This Principle embodies the truth that
"All is Mind." It explains that THE
ALL (which is the Substantial Reality
underlying all the outward manifestations
and appearances which we know under the
terms of "The Material Universe"; the
"Phenomena of Life"; "Matter"; "Energy"; and, in short, all that is apparent
to our material senses) is SPIRIT, which
in itself is UNKNOWABLE and UNDE-
FINABLE, but which may be considered
and thought of as AN UNIVERSAL, IN-

FINITE, LIVING MIND. It also explains that all the phenomenal world or universe is simply a Mental Creation of THE ALL, subject to the Laws of Created Things, and that the universe, as a whole, and in its parts or units, has its existence in the Mind of THE ALL, in which Mind we "live and move and have our being." This Principle, by establishing the Mental Nature of the Universe, easily explains all of the varied mental and psychic phenomena that occupy such a large portion of the public attention, and which, without such explanation, are non-understandable and defy scientific treatment. An understanding of this great Hermetic Principle of Mentalism enables the individual to readily grasp the laws of the Mental Universe, and to apply the same to his well-being and advancement. The Hermetic Student is enabled to apply intelligently the great Mental Laws, instead of using them in a haphazard manner. With the Master-Key in his possession, the student may unlock the many doors of the mental and psychic temple of knowledge, and enter the same freely and intelligently. This Principle explains the true nature of "Energy," "Power," and "Matter," and why and how all these are subordinate to the Mastery of Mind. One of the old Hermetic Masters wrote, long ages ago: "He who grasps the truth of the Mental Nature of the Universe is well advanced on The Path to Mastery." And these words are as true to-day as at the time they were first written. Without this Master-Key, Mastery is impossible, and the student knocks in vain at the many doors of The Temple.

II.   THE PRINCIPLE OF CORRESPONDENCE.

"As above, so below; as below, so above."—*The Kybalion.*

This Principle embodies the truth that there is always a Correspondence between the laws and phenomena of the various planes of Being and Life. The old Hermetic axiom ran in these words: "As above, so below; as below, so above." And

the grasping of this Principle gives one
the means of solving many a dark paradox,
and hidden secret of Nature.   There are
planes beyond our knowing, but when we
apply the Principle of Correspondence to
them we are able to understand much that
would otherwise be unknowable to us. This
Principle is of universal application and
manifestation, on the various planes of the
material, mental, and spiritual universe—
it is an Universal Law.   The ancient Hermetists considered this Principle as one of
the most important mental instruments by
which man was able to pry aside the obsta-
cles which hid from view the Unknown.
Its use even tore aside the Veil of Isis to
the extent that a glimpse of the face of the
goddess might be caught. Just as a knowledge of the Principles of Geometry enables
man to measure distant suns and their
movements, while seated in his observa-
tory, so a knowledge of the Principle of
Correspondence enables Man to reason intelligently from the Known to the Un-

known.   Studying the monad, he understands the archangel.

III.   THE PRINCIPLE OF VIBRATION.

"Nothing rests; everything moves; everything vibrates."—*The Kybalion.*

This Principle embodies the truth that
"everything is in motion"; "everything
vibrates"; "nothing is at rest"; facts
which Modern Science endorses, and which
each new scientific discovery tends to ver-
ify.   And yet this Hermetic Principle was
enunciated thousands of years ago, by the
Masters of Ancient Egypt.   This Principle explains that the differences between
different manifestations of Matter, Energy, Mind, and even Spirit, result largely
from varying rates of Vibration.   From
THE ALL, which is Pure Spirit, down to
the grossest form of Matter, all is in vibration—the higher the vibration, the higher
the position in the scale.   The vibration of
Spirit is at such an infinite rate of inten-
sity and rapidity that it is practically at

rest—just as a rapidly moving wheel seems
to be motionless. And at the other end of
the scale, there are gross forms of matter
whose vibrations are so low as to seem at
rest. Between these poles, there are millions upon millions of varying degrees of
vibration. From corpuscle and electron,
atom and molecule, to worlds and uni-
verses, everything is in vibratory motion.
This is also true on the planes of energy
and force (which are but varying degrees
of vibration); and also on the mental
planes (whose states depend upon vibrations); and even on to the spiritual planes.
An understanding of this Principle, with
the appropriate formulas, enables Hermetic students to control their own mental
vibrations as well as those of others. The
Masters also apply this Principle to the
conquering of Natural phenomena, in various ways. "He who understands the Principle of Vibration, has grasped the sceptre
of power," says one of the old writers.

IV. THE PRINCIPLE OF POLARITY.

"Everything is Dual; everything has poles; every-thing has its pair of opposites; like and unlike are the same; opposites are identical in nature, but different in degree; extremes meet; all truths are but half-truths; all paradoxes may be reconciled."—*The Kybalion.*

This Principle embodies the truth that "everything is dual"; "everything has two poles"; "everything has its pair of opposites," all of which were old Hermetic axioms. It explains the old paradoxes, that have perplexed so many, which have been stated as follows: "Thesis and anti-thesis are identical in nature, but different in degree"; "opposites are the same, dif-fering only in degree"; "the pairs of op-posites may be reconciled"; "extremes meet"; "everything is and isn't, at the same time"; "all truths are but half-truths"; "every truth is half-false"; "there are two sides to everything," etc., etc., etc. It explains that in everything there are two poles, or opposite aspects, and that "opposites" are really only the two extremes of the same thing, with **many** varying degrees between them. To illustrate: Heat and Cold, although "opposites," are really the same thing, the differences consisting merely of degrees of the same thing. Look at your thermometer and see if you can discover where "heat" terminates and "cold" begins! There is no such thing as "absolute heat" or "absolute cold"—the two terms "heat" and "cold" simply indicate varying degrees of the same thing, and that "same thing" which manifests as "heat" and "cold" is merely a form, variety, and rate of Vibration. So "heat" and "cold" are simply the "two poles" of that which we call "Heat"—and the phenomena attendant thereupon are manifestations of the Principle of Polarity. The same Principle manifests in the case of "Light and Darkness," which are the same thing, the difference consisting of varying degrees between the two poles of the phenomena. Where does "darkness" leave off, and "light" begin? What is the difference between "Large and Small"? Between

"Hard and Soft"? Between "Black and White"? Between "Sharp and Dull"? Between "Noise and Quiet"? Between "High and Low"? Between "Positive and Negative"? The Principle of Polarity explains these paradoxes, and no other Principle can supersede it. The same Principle operates on the Mental Plane. Let us take a radical and extreme example— that of "Love and Hate," two mental states apparently totally different. And yet there are degrees of Hate and degrees of Love, and a middle point in which we use the terms "Like or Dislike," which shade into each other so gradually that sometimes we are at a loss to know whether we "like" or "dislike" or "neither." And all are simply degrees of the same thing, as you will see if you will but think a moment. And, more than this (and considered of more importance by the Hermetists), it is possible to change the vibrations of Hate to the vibrations of Love, in one's own mind, and in the minds of others. Many of you, who read these lines, have had personal experiences of the involuntary rapid transition from Love to Hate, and the reverse, in your own case and that of others. And you will therefore realize the possibility of this being accomplished by the use of the Will, by means of the Hermetic formulas. "Good and Evil" are but the poles of the same thing, and the Hermetist understands the art of transmuting Evil into Good, by means of an application of the Principle of Polarity. In short, the "Art of Polarization" becomes a phase of "Mental Alchemy" known and practiced by the ancient and modern Hermetic Masters. An understanding of the Principle will enable one to change his own Polarity, as well as that of others, if he will devote the time and study necessary to master the art.

V. THE PRINCIPLE OF RHYTHM.

"Everything flows, out and in; everything has its tides; all things rise and fall; the pendulum-swing manifests in everything; the measure of the swing to the right is the measure of the swing to the left; rhythm compensates."—*The Kybalion.*

This Principle embodies the truth that in everything there is manifested a measured motion, to and fro; a flow and inflow; a swing backward and forward; a pendulum-like movement; a tide-like ebb and flow; a high-tide and low-tide; between the two poles which exist in accordance with the Principle of Polarity described a moment ago. There is always an action and a reaction; an advance and a retreat; a rising and a sinking. This is in the affairs of the Universe, suns, worlds, men, animals, mind, energy, and matter. This law is manifest in the creation and destruction of worlds; in the rise and fall of nations; in the life of all things; and finally in the mental states of Man (and it is with this latter that the Hermetists find the understanding of the Principle most important). The Hermetists have grasped this Principle, finding its universal application, and have also discovered certain means to overcome its effects in themselves by the use of the appropriate formulas and methods. They apply the Mental Law of

Neutralization. They cannot annul the Principle, or cause it to cease its operation, but they have learned how to escape its effects upon themselves to a certain degree depending upon the Mastery of the Principle. They have learned how to USE it, instead of being USED BY it. In this and similar methods, consist the Art of the Hermetists. The Master of Hermetics polarizes himself at the point at which he desires to rest, and then neutralizes the Rhythmic swing of the pendulum which would tend to carry him to the other pole. All individuals who have attained any degree of Self-Mastery do this to a certain degree, more or less unconsciously, but the Master does this consciously, and by the use of his Will, and attains a degree of Poise and Mental Firmness almost impossible of belief on the part of the masses who are swung backward and forward like a pendulum. This Principle and that of Polarity have been closely studied by the Hermetists, and the methods of counteracting, neutralizing, and USING them form an important part of the Hermetic Mental Alchemy.

VI.   THE PRINCIPLE OF CAUSE AND EFFECT.

"Every Cause has its Effect; every Effect has its Cause; everything happens according to Law; Chance is but a name for Law not recognized; there are many planes of causation, but nothing escapes the Law."— *The Kybalion.*

This Principle embodies the fact that there is a Cause for every Effect; an Effect from every Cause. It explains that: "Everything Happens according to Law"; that nothing ever "merely happens"; that there is no such thing as Chance; that while there are various planes of Cause and Effect, the higher dominating the lower planes, still nothing ever entirely escapes the Law. The Hermetists understand the art and methods of rising above the ordinary plane of Cause and Effect, to a certain degree, and by mentally rising to a higher plane they become Causers instead of Effects. The masses of people are carried along, obedient to environ-

ment; the wills and desires of others
stronger than themselves; heredity; sug-
gestion; and other outward causes moving
them about like pawns on the Chessboard
of Life. But the Masters, rising to the
plane above, dominate their moods, char-
acters, qualities, and powers, as well as the
environment surrounding them, and become Movers instead of pawns. They help
to PLAY THE GAME OF LIFE, instead
of being played and moved about by other
wills and environment. They USE the
Principle instead of being its tools. The
Masters obey the Causation of the higher
planes, but they help to RULE on their
own plane. In this statement there is con-
densed a wealth of Hermetic knowledge—
let him read who can.

VII.   THE PRINCIPLE OF GENDER.

"Gender is in everything; everything has its Masculine and Feminine Principles; Gender manifests on all
planes."—*The Kybalion.*

VII.   THE PRINCIPLE OF GENDER.

This Principle embodies the truth that

there is GENDER manifested in everything—the Masculine and Feminine Principles ever at work. This is true not only
of the Physical Plane, but of the Mental
and even the Spiritual Planes. On the
Physical Plane, the Principle manifests as
SEX, on the higher planes it takes higher
forms, but the Principle is ever the same.
No creation, physical, mental or spiritual,
is possible without this Principle. An understanding of its laws will throw light
on many a subject that has perplexed the
minds of men. The Principle of Gender
works ever in the direction of generation,
regeneration, and creation. Everything,
and every person, contains the two Ele-
ments or Principles, or this great Principle, within it, him or her. Every Male
thing has the Female Element also; every
Female contains also the Male Principle.
If you would understand the philosophy of
Mental and Spiritual Creation, Generation,
and Re-generation, you must understand
and study this Hermetic Principle. It contains the solution of many mysteries of

Life. We caution you that this Principle
has no reference to the many base, per-
nicious and degrading lustful theories,
teachings and practices, which are taught
under fanciful titles, and which are a
prostitution of the great natural principle
of Gender. Such base revivals of the ancient infamous forms of Phallicism tend to
ruin mind, body and soul, and the Hermetic
Philosophy has ever sounded the warning
note against these degraded teachings
which tend toward lust, licentiousness, and
perversion of Nature's principles. If you
seek such teachings, you must go elsewhere
for them—Hermeticism contains nothing
for you along these lines. To the pure, all
things are pure; to the base, all things are
base.

CPSIA information can be obtained
at www.ICGtesting.com
Printed in the USA
LVHW061916140723
752400LV00017B/15